OUTSTANDING AFRICAN AMERICANS

GREAT AFRICAN AMERICANS IN

ENTERTAINMENT

PAT REDIGER

Crabtree Publishing Company

Dedication

This series is dedicated to the African-American men and women who dared to follow their dreams. With courage, faith, and hard work, they overcame obstacles in their lives and went on to excel in their fields. They fought for civil rights and encouraged hope and self-reliance. They celebrated the glory of the athlete and the joy of knowledge and learning. They brought entertainment, poetry, and song to the world, and we are richer for it. *Outstanding African Americans* is both an acknowledgement of and a tribute to these people.

Project Manager
Amanda Woodrow

Writing Team
Karen Dudley
Pat Rediger

Editor
Virginia Mainprize

Research
Karen Dudley

Design and layout
Warren Clark
Karen Dudley

Photograph Credits
Archive Photos: pages 5 (Popperfoto), 10, 17, 19 (Frank Capri/SAGA), 22, 23 (American Stock), 26, 28 (Schiff/SAGA), 32, 33, 38, 41, 43, 49, 52, 55, 58 (Popperfoto); **Reuters/Bettman:** page 44; **UPI/Bettman:** pages 7, 8, 9, 42; **Blackstar:** pages 12 (McCoy), 37 (Blankenhorn); **Canapress Photo Service:** pages 20, 31, 61; **Frank Driggs Collection, courtesy of the Afro-American Historical and Cultural Museum:** page 14; **Globe Photos:** pages 11, 13, 40, 45; **Ponopresse Internationale Inc.:** pages 29, 31, 35; **Retna Ltd:** pages 16 (Martin), 21 (Sarvary), 25 (Redfern), 27 (Stromme/Stills), 34 (Martin), 36, 39 (Johnson); **Schomburg Center for Research in Black Culture, The New York Public Library, Astor, Lenox and Tilden Foundations:** pages 4, 6; **Urban Archives, Temple University:** page 24; **Woodfin Camp & Associates:** pages 15 (Press), 18 (Chenet).

Published by
Crabtree Publishing Company

350 Fifth Avenue,	360 York Road, R.R. 4	73 Lime Walk
Suite 3308	Niagara-on-the-Lake,	Headington
New York, New York	Ontario Canada	Oxford Ox3 7AD
U.S.A. 10018	L0S 1J0	United Kingdom

Cataloging-in-Publication Data

Rediger, Pat, 1966-
  Great African Americans in entertainment/by Pat Rediger.
    p. cm. —(Outstanding African Americans series)
  Includes index.
  Summary. Examines the lives of more than ten African American entertainers, including Josephine Baker, Sammy Davis, Jr., Susan Taylor, and Spike Lee, with the obstacles they each overcame.
    ISBN 0-86505-799-0 (lib. bdg.)—ISBN 0-86505-813-X (pbk.)
  1. Afro-American entertainers—Biography—Juvenile literture. 2. Afro-american singers—Biography—Juvenile literature. [1. Entertainers. 2. Singers. 3. Afro-Americans—Biography.] I. Title. II Series: Rediger, Pat, 1966- Outstanding African Americans series.
  PN2286.R44 1996
  791'.08996073—dc20   95-37451
                                                          CIP
                                                          AC

Contents

KN

Josephine Baker

Personality Profile

Career: Singer, dancer, and entertainer.

Born: June 3, 1906, in St. Louis, Missouri, to Eddie Carson and Carrie McDonald.

Died: April 14, 1975, in Paris, France.

Education: Dropped out of school at age thirteen.

Family: Married Willie Wells, 1918, divorced; married William Baker, 1921, divorced; married Guiseppe Abatino, 1927, later died; married Jean Lion, 1937, divorced; married Jo Bouillon, 1947, separated and later died; married Robert Brady, 1973, divorced. Had twelve adopted children, Akio, Janot, Jari, Luis, Jean-Claude, Moise, Marianne, Brahim, Koffi, Mara, Noel, and Stellina.

Awards: Croix de Guerre; Rosette de la Résistance; Legion d'Honneur for International Understanding, 1968; Presidential Medal of Freedom, 1977.

Growing Up

imes were tough for Josephine when she was growing up in St. Louis, Missouri. She was abandoned by her father, and her stepfather was often violent. Her family suffered from extreme poverty. In 1914, by the time Josephine was eight, she was working as a maid for white families. Josephine soon learned that she must rely on herself.

Even as a child, Josephine loved to perform. She and her friends put on shows for the children of the neighborhood, and Josephine was always the star.

Before her fourteenth birthday, Josephine ran away from home and got a job as a waitress. She married Willie Wells but left him soon after the wedding.

Josephine wanted to go into show business. When she was fifteen, she joined the Jones Family Band, a group of street performers who were later known as the Dixie Fliers. Josephine was a dresser who helped the star change into her costumes.

"In my wildest dreams then, I could not have believed what would happen to me."

The next year, one of the chorus girls got hurt, so Josephine took her place. Josephine's energy and her talent for comedy impressed audiences. She could perform the most complicated dance steps while crossing her eyes. While on tour with the Dixie Fliers, Josephine met and married William Baker.

Developing Skills

J osephine moved to New York and got a part in the touring company of the musical *Shuffle Along*. She was turned down for the New York production because she was not yet sixteen.

When she was performing in the chorus at the Plantation Club in Harlem, New York, Josephine met Caroline Dudley, a wealthy producer who convinced her to join a black dance group traveling to France. The company received rave reviews, and soon Josephine was the featured performer in the most popular dance number. She became the hit of Paris.

In 1926, when she was twenty, Josephine joined the Folies Bergère, the main Paris music hall. She was immensely popular, and her hairstyle started a fashion craze. Josephine dolls and perfume also appeared in elegant Paris shops. Soon she opened her own night club.

In 1936, Josephine decided to go back to the United States and dance in the *Ziegfeld Follies*. Although she was accepted everywhere in Paris, Josephine faced racism as soon as she returned to America. A grand hotel in New York offered her a free suite. But she was asked to leave by a back door because some whites might have objected to a black person staying at the hotel. Josephine returned to France.

This is a 1936 poster advertising one of Josephine's shows.

After World War II, Josephine married a French orchestra leader, Jo Bouillon. Together, they restored a large castle in the French countryside and opened it to tourists. It included two hotels, three restaurants, a miniature golf course, a wax museum, stables, a gas station, a post office, and more. While she lived there, Josephine adopted twelve children from different ethnic backgrounds.

Josephine hoped to pay her many bills with money from the tourists and her performances. But the bills mounted, and, in 1969, Josephine was evicted from her castle. Princess Grace of Monaco heard about Josephine's situation and bought her a house in the south of France. Josephine got what work she could, but sometimes she had to beg in the streets for her children.

In 1974, Josephine starred in *Joséphine*. She was almost seventy years old but was on the stage for the whole show. The show was sold out every night. Six days after opening night, Josephine suffered a stroke and died the next morning.

Josephine in one of the many gowns she took with her on a tour of South America in 1939.

Accomplishments

1925 Performed with La Revue Nègre in Paris, France.	**1936** Performed with the *Ziegfeld Follies* in the United States.
1926 Joined the Folies Bergère, the top Paris music hall.	**1942** Performed for Allied troops during the war.
1934 Starred in the movie *Zou-Zou* and the opera *La Créole*.	**1973** Appeared at Carnegie Hall.
	1974 Starred in *Joséphine*.

Overcoming Obstacles

Josephine was a woman who did not let obstacles stand in her way. She was not a great dancer when she first started in show business. She tripped over her feet and was often out-of-step. She took dancing lessons and watched other dancers to learn their routines. Soon she was getting rave reviews.

In 1936, Josephine returned to the United States for the first time in ten years.

Josephine's strong personality helped her succeed. She always realized the importance of getting people to notice her. Once she advertized her new show by walking a baby leopard wearing a diamond collar along the main streets of Paris.

After being a hit in Paris, Josephine hoped to find equal success in the United States. When she returned there in 1936, she spent months practicing for her role in the *Ziegfeld Follies*, but reviewers hated the show. It seemed that most Americans were not ready to accept an African-American woman as a star.

"I have always taken the rocky path. I never took the easy one, but as I grew older, and as I knew I had the power and the strength, I took that rocky path, and I tried to smooth it out a little."

Josephine made a return trip to the United States in 1951. She toured the country but refused to perform in clubs that would not allow African Americans in the audience. This time Josephine was a great success, and the people of Harlem turned out to honor her on Josephine Baker Day.

During World War II, Josephine was a French spy, passing on military secrets to help end the war. When the war moved closer to France, Josephine moved to Morocco where she performed for French, British, and American soldiers. For her war efforts, Josephine was given two of France's highest awards.

Josephine often wore fancy costumes in her shows.

In 1963, Josephine took part in the historic March on Washington when more than 200,000 people marched on the nation's capital for civil rights. Josephine spoke to them about her struggle to succeed as a black, female performer.

Josephine was a dedicated showperson all her life. Despite poor health for the last ten years of her life, she kept on performing. During her last show, *Joséphine*, she had more energy than anyone else and danced every night on stage even though she was almost seventy.

Special Interests

- Josephine loved animals and would often travel with her parrot, rabbits, and a snake. She had a pet leopard which she walked on the main streets of Paris.
- In 1954, Josephine decided she wanted a family. Over the next eight years, she adopted twelve children from all races. She called them her Rainbow Tribe.

Harry Belafonte

Personality Profile

Career: Singer and actor.

Born: March 1, 1927, in New York, New York, to Harold and Melvine Belafonte.

Education: Dramatic Workshop of the New School for Social Research.

Family: Married Marguerite Byrd, 1948, divorced; married Julie Robinson, 1957. Has four children, Adrienne, Shari, David, and Gina.

Awards: Tony Award, 1953; Emmy award, 1960; Martin Luther King, Jr. Nonviolent Peace Prize, 1982; Recipient ABAA Music Award for efforts to aid African famine victims and for producing the album and video *We Are the World*, 1985; Grammy award, 1985; Kennedy Center Honors for Lifetime Achievement in the Performing Arts, 1989; Thurgood Marshall Lifetime Achievement Award, 1993; National Medal of Arts Award, NAACP, 1994; several honorary degrees.

Growing Up

When Harry was born in 1927, his West Indian parents lived in Harlem, New York. Here Harry saw his father's dignity destroyed by unemployment, and he watched in helpless anger when his mother, a domestic servant, was slapped in the face by her white employer. At age eight, Harry and his family moved to Jamaica to live in the house where his mother had been raised.

At that time, Jamaica was under British rule, and young Harry saw first-hand how poorly the native Jamaicans were treated by the white British. But Jamaica also taught Harry about the power of music. He often heard native Jamaicans singing to relieve the stresses of living in a racist society. It was a lesson that Harry would not forget.

When he was thirteen, Harry and his family moved back to Harlem seeking a better life. But things did not improve much. Harry's father had trouble finding a job, and he became depressed because he was unable to support his family.

In Harlem, Harry attended school until age seventeen when he joined the U.S. Navy. After his tour of duty ended, Harry returned to New York and got a job as a janitor in an apartment building. One day, one of the building's tenants gave Harry two tickets for a play at the American Negro Theater. The play would change Harry's life.

"The environment [in Jamaica] was terribly musical. People sang while working in the fields, while selling their wares in the streets, in church, during festivals. That background had a great impact on me."

Developing Skills

hen Harry saw his first play at the American Negro Theater, he was fascinated. He knew immediately he wanted to become an actor.

Harry enrolled in the Dramatic Workshop to study acting. As a class project, he sang a song he had written called "Recognition." The owner of a popular jazz club, the Royal Roost, was in the audience. He recognized Harry's talent and offered him a two-week job singing at the club. Harry's performance was so popular that the two weeks were extended to twenty. After this success, Harry spent the next two years singing in night clubs across America.

Although Harry continued to sing he also followed his dream of becoming an actor. Over the next few decades, he acted in plays, on television, and in films such as *Carmen Jones* and *Uptown Saturday Night*.

Harry performing in 1965.

But it is for his music that Harry is best known. In 1956, Harry released the album *Calypso*. The songs on this album used melodies and rhythms from Jamaica. When American audiences heard these songs, they fell in love with Caribbean music. *Calypso* sold more than one million copies — the first album ever to do so.

Harry was especially interested in folk music. He hired someone to travel across the United States taping old folk songs from the cotton fields, river plantations, and prisons. Harry also collected the folk music of other cultures, but his calypso songs remain the most popular. His most famous recording is the "Banana Boat Song."

"I love being an artist; it is my first joy."

Harry performs with Joan Baez, Chrissy Hynde, and Keith Richards at the Live Aid benefit concert in 1985.

Accomplishments

1946 Began singing at the Royal Roost jazz club.

1953 Appeared in the film *Bright Road* and the play *John Murray Anderson's Almanac*.

1955 Appeared in the film *Carmen Jones*.

1956 Released the album *Calypso*.

1985 Produced *We Are the World* album and video.

1987 Appointed a UNICEF goodwill ambassador.

1988 Released album *Paradise in Gazankulu*.

Overcoming Obstacles

fter Harry's first success singing in clubs, he found that many night club owners wanted him to sing only jazz music. But Harry was more interested in folk singing.

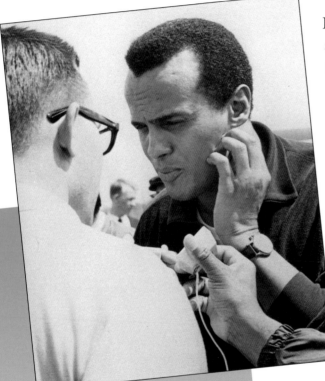

In 1965, Harry participated in the Selma to Montgomery march in which over 50,000 people marched to Montgomery, Alabama, to protest against interference with voting rights for African Americans.

Harry believed that he could combine his singing and acting skills to become a successful folk singer. He cancelled all his appointments in jazz night clubs and lost a lot of money by doing this. Harry collected many old and new songs, spending hours listening to records he had borrowed from the library. After memorizing many of these folk ballads, Harry had to find night clubs that would hire him. These clubs did not know who Harry was, and he still had to prove to them that he would draw in the audiences. At first, Harry made very little money, but, in time, his singing talent was recognized.

Harry was asked to perform in the movie *Carmen Jones*, a musical that starred many African Americans. But the producers did not think that Harry was a good enough singer. Whenever Harry sang in the movie, his voice was replaced by an opera singer's voice. Many critics liked Harry's acting, and, because of his performance, he was able to get other acting jobs in which he was allowed to sing.

Despite his success, Harry never forgot the racism of his youth. Even though he had an extremely busy and successful career, he always made time to fight for human and civil rights. He was a close friend of Martin Luther King, Jr. and helped organize Martin's famous March on Washington for civil rights. Sometimes he was able to use his talents to help underprivileged people, as he did in 1985 with his *We Are the World* record album. The proceeds from this album went to fight poverty and hunger.

After his long and successful performing career, Harry thought that he would be able to retire and relax. He wanted to visit Tibet and the Mayan ruins in Central America. But Harry could not sit back and rest while there was still so much racism and poverty in the world. He continued his ongoing fight for human rights. In 1987, Harry became the Goodwill Ambassador for UNICEF (the United Nation's Children Fund).

In 1995, Harry traveled to Rwanda, Africa, as part of his on-going fight for human rights.

Special Interests

- One of Harry's hobbies is designing and building furniture. He also enjoys assembling stereo equipment.
- Harry is a fan of the New York Knickerbockers basketball team.
- Harry is active in the civil rights movement. He was arrested outside the South African Embassy in Washington, D.C. Harry was protesting against the country's racist government. He also sang at South African president Nelson Mandela's seventieth birthday.

Bill Cosby

Personality Profile

Career: Comedian, television and film star.

Born: July 12, 1937, in Philadelphia, Pennsylvania, to William and Anna Cosby.

Family: Married Camille Hanks, 1964. Has five children, Erika, Erinne, Ennis, Ensa, and Evin.

Education: M.A., Ed.D., University of Massachusetts, 1977.

Awards: Eight Grammy awards; five Emmy awards; NAACP Image Award.

Growing Up

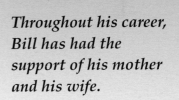

Bill was born and raised in the black ghetto of Philadelphia known as the Jungle. The pressures of work and of supporting a growing family took their toll on Bill's father. He began drinking and disappearing for long periods.

When Bill was about ten years old, his father abandoned the family and joined the navy. Bill's mother worked for twelve hours a day cleaning other people's homes. Bill was left to be both mother and father to his two younger brothers. He got up each day at sunrise to sell fruit or shine shoes before going to school. After school he had to come home and look after his brothers.

Throughout his career, Bill has had the support of his mother and his wife.

But there were good times too. Mrs. Cosby had a wonderful sense of humor. She loved to read to her boys, and Bill especially enjoyed stories about the adventures of Huckleberry Finn. When Bill became a comedian, he would tell stories about his family. The stories were funny, and Bill never mentioned the pain of those difficult years.

Bill used to play football on the street. He and his friends would stuff crumpled newspapers inside their shirts to look like shoulder pads. When he got to junior high school, Bill joined the school football team and played so well that he was made team captain. He was also made captain of the track and field team.

"The only thing I [Bill's mother] had to give him was plenty of love, and oh, dear God, I gave him all I had. But success comes from within, and Bill was determined to be something."

Bill quit school after he failed grade ten and joined the U.S. Navy. When his term ended four years later, Bill enrolled at Temple University on an athletic scholarship.

Bill's first experience with comedy was when he was a boy watching programs on his friend's television. Bill saw all the famous comedians of that time, and he dreamed of one day performing with them.

As Bill grew up, his sense of humor grew sharper. By the time he was at Temple University, he was spending his evenings performing in the comedy clubs. Bill was so successful that he left university after his junior year and moved to Greenwich Village in New York City to find work. Bill was different from other comedians because he told jokes about everyday life. Since most of his audiences were made up of everyday people, he was very popular.

In 1963, Bill appeared on the "Tonight Show," a late-night television talk show. Producer Sheldon Leonard spotted Bill on the show and was impressed with his talent. Sheldon was planning a new show called "I Spy" about two American spies. Sheldon asked Bill to be one of the leads. It was the first time an African American had been given a starring role on television. The show was a hit.

Bill on the set of "The "Cosby Show."

"As for involvement, I'm emotionally involved with life."

When "I Spy" was cancelled, Bill began a new show about a physical education teacher at a Los Angeles high school. Named "The Bill Cosby Show," the story took place in a lower-middle-class neighborhood. The show was well watched during its first year, but viewers dropped off in the second year and the show was cancelled.

In 1972, Bill returned to television to tell stories about the people from his childhood in a cartoon show titled "Fat Albert and the Cosby Kids." He released several very popular comedy albums and appeared in such films as *The Devil and Max Devlin* and *Uptown Saturday Night*. He also appeared in many television commercials.

Bill's most successful television show, "The Cosby Show," began in 1984. This comedy about an African-American doctor and his family became the number-one program across the country, remaining in the top spot until 1989. The show ended in 1992.

Bill in front of a display of his book, **Childhood,** *which he published in 1991.*

Accomplishments

1965 Starred in "I Spy."	**1984** "The Cosby Show" began.
1969 "The Bill Cosby Show" began.	**1986** Published *Bill Cosby's Personal Guide to Tennis Power* and *Fatherhood*.
1972 Voice on the cartoon series "Fat Albert and the Cosby Kids," appeared on "The Electric Co."	**1990** Starred in *Ghost Dad*.
1974 Starred in *Uptown Saturday Night*.	**1991** Published *Childhood*.
1979 Starred in *The Devil and Max Devlin*.	**1994** "The Cosby Mysteries" began.

W hen Bill's father left the family, Bill became responsible for his younger brothers. Bill's mother had to work twelve-hour days just to make ends meet, so Bill looked after his brothers and cooked the breakfasts. Bill dealt with this responsibility by making jokes and clowning around. He always tried to make the food more fun by adding food coloring. He and his brothers often ate purple and orange waffles and green or blue scrambled eggs.

As a youth, Bill had problems in school. Intelligence testing indicated that he was quite smart, but, instead of paying attention to the teacher, Bill often joked around and ignored his studies. When he failed grade ten, Bill decided to drop out of school. While he was in the navy, he took correspondence classes and got his high school diploma. In 1975, he returned to college, earning a master's degree and then a doctorate in education.

In 1987, Bill helped launch a campaign to free political prisoners in South Africa.

Bill's big break in the entertainment world came during "I Spy." But some African Americans criticized him for taking the role because they felt his character in the show did not show an ordinary African American. Bill did not let this criticism upset him. He told his critics that "I Spy" was not about the problems of black people, and that his character was just another human being.

Bill's television shows have not always been successful. During the 1970s, he was featured in two new shows which lasted only a year. Several of the major television networks lost faith in Bill, and when he tried to sell them the idea for another show in 1984, most of them turned him down. Only NBC agreed to try "The Cosby Show." The show was a huge success.

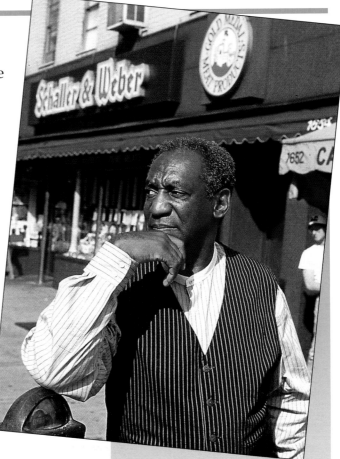

Bill on the set of "The Cosby Mysteries" in 1994.

Special Interests

- Bill is interested in education and spent several years working for the Children's Television Network. He also donated $20 million to Spelman College in Atlanta.
- Bill has written several books including *The Wit and Wisdom of Fat Albert, Bill Cosby's Personal Guide to Tennis Power, Fatherhood,* and *Time Flies.*
- Bill has been active in the Rhythm & Blues Hall of Fame and has served as president since 1968.

Sammy Davis, Jr.

Personality Profile

Career: Singer, dancer, comedian, and actor.

Born: December 8, 1925, in Harlem, New York, to Sam, Sr. and Elvera Davis.

Died: May 16, 1990, in Los Angeles, California.

Education: No formal schooling.

Family: Married Loray White, 1959, (divorced 1960); married Mai Britt, 1961, (divorced 1968); married Altovise Gore, 1970. Had three children, Tracey, Mark, and Jeff.

Awards: Winner of numerous awards including: Record of the Year, *Metronome*, 1946; Most Outstanding New Personality of the Year, *Metronome*, 1946; Entertainer of the Year, *Cue*, 1964; Spingarn Medal, NAACP, 1968; honored by the National Academy of Television Arts and Sciences, 1974; Life Achievement Award, the Friars Club, 1974; Sammy Davis, Jr. Drive dedicated in Chicago, 1990.

Growing Up

It seems that Sammy was born with show business in his blood. His parents, Sam and Elvera, were members of a black vaudeville troupe, a stage show that traveled around the country entertaining audiences with songs, dances, and impersonations of well-known people.

Sammy was raised as a baby in Harlem by his grandmother. His parents separated when he was two-and-a-half and Sammy went to live with his father and the vaudeville troupe. He liked to copy his father and uncle and the other singers and dancers when they were rehearsing. Soon the manager of the act noticed his talent. In 1929, though he was only four years old, Sammy was made a part of the act.

"Packing suitcases and riding on trains and buses were as natural to me as a stroll in a carriage might be to another child. Although I had traveled ten states and played over fifty cities by the time I was four, I never felt I was without a home."

During the Depression, Sammy's father and uncle left the group and formed a trio which included little Sammy. They spent most of their time on the road, playing in cities and small towns. Often they were so broke they did not have enough money to scrape together the train fare to move to the next town. Sammy never really went to school. His father tried to find people in the theaters where the trio performed to teach Sammy in their spare time.

Sammy was only six years old when he starred in his first movie, *Rufus Jones for President.* In this comedy, Sammy played the lead role of a little boy who falls asleep and dreams he is the President of the United States.

W hen he turned eighteen, Sammy was drafted into the army and placed in the Special Services Division. The Division provided entertainment for the soldiers, and Sammy sang and danced at army camps across the country. He also wrote, directed, and produced some of the camp shows.

Sammy performing in 1957.

In 1945, Sammy left the army to rejoin his father's vaudeville act. Vaudeville was no longer popular, and few places would hire the trio. Sammy spent his spare time in night clubs watching other acts and making new friends. One of them helped him record the song "The Way You Look Tonight." The music magazine *Metronome* named it the record of the year and called Sammy the most outstanding new personality of 1946.

The trio changed their act, and Sammy became the star while his uncle and father sang and danced in the background. They were now asked to perform in many important night clubs. Sammy also began recording his songs and impersonations of famous people.

In 1956, Sammy made his first appearance on Broadway, the New York theater area. He starred in a comedy called *Mr. Wonderful* which was created especially for Sammy. The show itself received bad reviews although Sammy's performance was praised.

In the late 1950s, Sammy first appeared in television variety shows without his father and uncle. Audiences loved watching Sammy sing and dance. He received more and more offers to appear on television and was even given his own shows.

Sammy's appearance in several movies, *Porgy and Bess* (1959) and *Robin and the Seven Hoods* (1964), also increased his popularity. In 1966, he wrote a best-selling autobiography, *Yes I Can*.

Sammy began to suffer from health problems in his fifties. He slowed his act down but managed to keep his humor and upbeat style. He continued to perform until his death in 1990.

From the 1950s until his death in 1990, Sammy performed on stage, in movies, and on television.

Accomplishments

1929 Joined vaudeville act with his father.

1931 Appeared in the movie *Rufus Jones for President*.

1943 Performed for the U.S. Army's Special Services Division.

1946 Recorded "The Way You Look Tonight."

1956 Appeared in the musical *Mr. Wonderful*.

1959 Appeared in the movie *Porgy and Bess*.

1964 Appeared in the movie *Robin and the Seven Hoods*.

1965 Wrote autobiography, *Yes, I Can*.

1966 Starred in the musical *Golden Boy*; starred in his own television show "The Sammy Davis, Jr. Show."

1974 Appeared in the act *Sammy on Broadway*.

1978 Appeared in the musical comedy *Stop the World, I Want to Get Off*.

Overcoming Obstacles

Because Sammy traveled across the country as a child, never staying long at any place, he never went to school. Even when he joined the army, he could hardly read. There, a fellow black soldier gave Sammy reading lessons, and Sammy discovered he loved books.

Sammy faced racism and the cruelty of white people for the first time when he served in the army. He did not know how to react. Once some soldiers painted his skin

with white paint. He tried to fight back with his fists, but the white soldiers beat him up. Finally Sammy realized that the only way to get respect from these men was through his performances. When faced with a racist audience, Sammy danced and sang with even more energy than usual. He wanted to show the white soldiers that he had talent and worth.

Throughout his career, Sammy faced racial prejudice when he dated white actresses. When he married Mai Britt, a Swedish actress, in 1961, he received death threats and hate mail.

"My talent was the weapon, the power, the way for me to fight [racism]. It was the only way I might hope to affect a man's thinking."

The years after World War II were probably the toughest for Sammy. People were not interested in vaudeville acts anymore, and it was hard to find work. Sammy knew that he had to change his act to keep the audiences entertained. He learned how to do impersonations of famous people and made his dance steps more difficult. He also learned to play the trumpet, drums, and piano. He became a performer with many talents, and the audiences loved his act.

Often called "Mr. Wonderful," Sammy could hold an audience's attention for hours with his unique style of entertaining.

In 1954, while performing in Las Vegas, Nevada, Sammy was asked to make a record album in Hollywood, California. On his way there, Sammy's car crashed into another vehicle. He was rushed to a hospital with head injuries, and the doctors had to remove his left eye. The accident changed Sammy. He adopted the Jewish faith to help him through this difficult time. A few weeks later, with an eye patch, Sammy was performing again. As he came out for his first show after the accident, the audience gave Sammy a ten-minute standing ovation.

Special Interests

- Sammy's favorite pastimes were photography, playing golf, and driving automobiles. He had a large collection of cars, including an expensive Rolls Royce.
- Sammy supported many worthwhile projects. He donated money and his talents for civil rights organizations. He hosted a twenty-one-hour television telethon for charity.

Whoopi Goldberg

Personality Profile

Career: Actor and comedian.

Born: 1950, in New York, New York, to Emma Johnson. Other sources state Whoopi was born in 1949, 1954, or 1955.

Education: Dropped out of high school at age seventeen.

Family: Married David Claessen, 1986, (divorced, 1988); married Lyle Trachtenberg, 1994. Has one daughter, Alexandrea Martin.

Awards: Golden Globe Award, 1985; Academy Award nomination, 1985; Image Award, NAACP, 1985, 1990; Grammy award, 1985; Kid's Choice Award, Nickelodeon, 1989; Humanitarian of the Year Award, Starlight Foundation, 1989; Academy Award, 1991; Female Star of the Year, National Association of Theater Owners, 1993; Woman of the Year, Harvard University's Hasty Pudding Theatricals, 1993; Favorite Actress in a Comedy Motion Picture, People's Choice Awards, 1994.

Growing Up

Whoopi may sound like an unusual name, but her parents actually called her Caryn Johnson, a name which Whoopi kept until she was in her twenties.

Whoopi grew up in a housing project in Manhattan, New York. Her father left when she was a child, and her mother had to work at many different jobs to support the family.

From a very early age, Whoopi was interested in acting. She loved watching romantic comedies and horror movies on television and dreamed of becoming an actor. When she was eight, Whoopi started to pursue her dream by acting in children's plays at the Hudson Guild Theater.

Whoopi in 1992 at the Cannes Film Festival in Cannes, France.

By age seventeen, Whoopi seemed to have lost touch with her dream. She dropped out of high school and began to take drugs. This lasted for two years until she decided to change her life. While she was kicking her drug addiction, Whoopi met and married her counsellor. Although the marriage did not last very long, Whoopi had a daughter, Alexandrea.

After her marriage ended, Whoopi decided she had to leave New York. She was a single mother and a high school dropout with no job prospects. Hoping to start over again, Whoopi moved to the West Coast to become an actor.

At that time, she changed her name from Caryn to Whoopi. Sometimes she called herself Whoopi Cushion and sometimes Whoopi Cushon, pretending she was French. Many people laughed at this strange name. Whoopi meant her name to be a joke, but, when she realized that no one would take her seriously with such a silly name, she added Goldberg, the name of one of her ancestors.

"Acting is the one thing I always knew I could do."

Whoopi's first big break came when she appeared in her own one-woman show where she played seventeen different roles. Her performance was a great success, and the show toured the country and traveled to Europe. Film director Steven Spielberg noticed her in one of her performances and was so impressed with her acting that he gave her the starring role in his movie *The Color Purple*. Whoopi played Celie, a victim of abuse. It was an incredible performance, and Whoopi received rave reviews and many awards.

After her success in *The Color Purple*, Whoopi was offered many other movie roles. She starred in *Jumpin' Jack Flash, Burglar,* and *The Telephone.* But most reviewers and audiences did not like these movies. Things changed in 1990 when Whoopi appeared in *Ghost*, the most successful film of that year.

Her career was back on track, and she appeared in *The Long Walk Home* and *Soap Dish.* Both of these movies were well received. Whoopi's recent films are *Sister Act* and *Boys on the Side.* She was also the voice of one of the hyenas in *The Lion King.*

In addition to movies, Whoopi has appeared on television where she plays Guinan, an occasional character on "Star Trek: The Next Generation."

Whoopi acting up with comedian Billy Crystal after the 1986 Grammy awards.

Accomplishments

1983 Opened the one-person drama *The Spook Show* on Broadway.

1985 Appeared in *The Color Purple.*

1986 Starred in *Jumpin' Jack Flash.*

1987 Starred in *Burglar.*

1990 Starred in *Ghost*, appeared on television series "Bagdad Cafe."

1990 Starred in *The Long Walk Home.*

1992 Starred in *Sister Act.*

1994 First African American to host the Academy Awards Show.

1995 Starred in *Boys on the Side.*

W hoopi was raised in a broken home where money was always scarce, and she spent much of her childhood wishing she were rich and white. She turned to laughter to cope with her troubles and found that telling jokes helped ease the pain. She loved to watch movies and pretend to be someone else. Even today, Whoopi has difficulty talking about her early life.

Whoopi after winning an Oscar for her role in **Ghost** *in 1991.*

Whoopi did not do well in school. Although she did not yet know it, she had a reading problem that made it hard for her to understand written words. Whoopi thought that she was just stupid. Frustrated, she dropped out of school at age seventeen and fell in with the wrong crowd. She took drugs for two years before finally realizing that she had to turn her life around. She went to a drug counsellor who helped her off the drugs, and she began to think about acting again.

"The greatest thing I was ever able to do was give a welfare check back. I brought it back to the welfare department and said, 'Here. I don't need this anymore.'"

But even though Whoopi knew she could be an actor, acting roles were scarce. She worked at many different jobs. She was a bricklayer, a bank teller, and even a hairstylist for a funeral home. To support herself and her daughter, Whoopi had to go on welfare for a while. The proudest moment of her life was when she could support herself and return her welfare money.

Whoopi starred in the film **Ghost** *with Patrick Swayze.*

Fame and success came with her role in *The Color Purple*, and Whoopi began receiving many job offers. But sometimes the roles she chose to play were not very good. Although she starred in *Jumpin' Jack Flash* and *Burglar*, the films were unsuccessful with both the critics and the public. All of a sudden, Whoopi found it difficult to get another role, and people began to say that her career was over.

In 1990, Whoopi turned this around with her performance in *Ghost*. The film was a huge hit, and Whoopi won the Oscar for Best Supporting Actress. With her career back on track, Whoopi now looks forward to future successes.

Special Interests

- Whoopi organizes the Comic Relief benefit shows on the television station HBO. These shows feature comedians such as Billy Crystal and Robin Williams. Money raised from the shows helps homeless people.
- Whoopi is noted for her hair braids. She calls them her "Do-do braids."
- Whoopi has a large collection of black dolls.

Spike Lee

Personality Profile

Career: Filmmaker and writer.

Born: March 20, 1957, in Atlanta, Georgia, to William and Jacqueline Lee.

Education: John Dewey High School; B.A., Morehouse College, 1979; M.A., New York University, 1983.

Family: Married Tonya Lewis, 1993. Has one daughter, Satchel.

Awards: Student Academy Award for *Joe's Bed-Stuy Barber Shop: We Cut Heads*, Academy of Motion Picture Arts and Sciences, 1982; New Generation Award, LA Film Critics for *She's Gotta Have It* ; Prix de Jeunesse, Cannes Film Festival for *She's Gotta Have It*, 1986.

Growing Up

Spike was the oldest of five children in his family. He was named Shelton but was nicknamed Spike by his mother, and the name stuck. Spike was born in Atlanta, Georgia, but, shortly after, his family moved to Chicago and then to New York. Spike's father made his living as a jazz bassist, and, for a while, the family lived comfortably. But the electric bass was becoming more popular, and Spike's father had trouble playing it. Job offers became fewer, and, during most of Spike's childhood, the family relied on the money that Spike's mother earned as a teacher.

Spike's mother took him to movies, museums, and art galleries. His father showed him how to play the guitar and piano. Spike often went to the jazz clubs to hear his father play bass.

When Spike graduated from high school, it seemed natural for him to attend Morehouse College, a mostly black college in Atlanta, Georgia. Both his father and grandfather had gone to Morehouse for their education. Spike loved college life and got involved in many activities. He wrote for the school newspaper and worked as a disc jockey at the local jazz radio station. During his second year at Morehouse, Spike began to take an interest in filmmaking.

Spike became interested in filmmaking while in his second year of college at Morehouse College.

Developing Skills

While still at Morehouse, Spike bought a movie camera and used it to make short films in his spare time. He graduated from Morehouse at age twenty-two and landed a summer job at Columbia Pictures in Burbank, California. Spike loved working at Columbia, and, when the summer ended, he decided to return to New York to study filmmaking at New York University. There he got a job as a teaching assistant and paid his tuition by working in the film equipment room. He spent the money his grandmother had given him for his college fees to make movies. Spike produced the film *Joe's Bed-Stuy Barbershop: We Cut Heads*. It won a student Academy Award and was shown on television and at international film festivals.

Hoping to find work as a movie director, Spike signed a contract with two talent agencies who promised to find him a movie job. But the agencies were unable to help Spike find any work. He supported himself for two years working for a company that sent movies to movie theaters. He realized that he would have to create his own projects to produce his own movies.

Spike in a film editing room.

In 1986, Spike wrote and directed *She's Gotta Have It*. The film was an instant hit and received a standing ovation at the San Francisco Film Festival. It also won the prize for best new film at the Cannes Film Festival and ended up making over $7 million in the theaters. Spike's career was on its way!

Over the next few years, Spike continued to make movies, and his reputation as a film director grew with each success. One of his films, *School Daze*, featured a special dance called "da butt." After the film was released, people started dancing "da butt" in night clubs across the country.

Spike on the set of **Jungle Fever** *in 1991.*

Spike's most expensive and popular film has been *X* which explored the life of civil rights leader Malcolm X. Spike is working on a film about the legendary African-American baseball player Jackie Robinson.

Accomplishments

1986 Wrote and directed *She's Gotta Have It.*	**1991** Wrote and directed *Jungle Fever.*
1988 Wrote and directed *School Daze.*	**1992** Taught classes on African-American film at Harvard University.
1989 Wrote and directed *Do the Right Thing.*	
1990 Wrote and directed *Mo' Better Blues,* and *X.*	**1994** Co-wrote and directed *Crooklyn.*
	1995 Released *Clockers.*

Overcoming Obstacles

Spike had trouble getting money for his movies. His first big movie attempt was *Messenger*. He had hired a cast and film crew and had asked the actors' union if he could pay the actors less than they would normally make. Usually the union agreed to this kind of request because they wanted to help small, independent producers make a name for themselves. In Spike's case they refused. The union said that, because his movie had a good chance of success, he should pay the actors their regular wage. Spike believed that the union did not support him because he was black. Spike was forced to cancel the film.

Spike wrote a new movie called *She's Gotta Have It*. He still did not have any funding and knew that he would have to make the movie with as little money as possible.

With just $18,000, Spike began filming. At the end of each day of filming, he would phone his friends and ask them to invest money in the movie. Every day, somebody would go to Spike's house to see if any checks had arrived. At one point, Spike owed the film processing company $2,000, and they told him that they would auction off his film if he did not pay. Fortunately, one of Spike's friends gave him the money to pay his bill and to keep working on the movie. The movie was shot in twelve days.

Spike had problems getting enough money together to make his first films. Even today, he sometimes gets friends to invest in his films.

When *She's Gotta Have It* became a huge success, Spike's determination was rewarded, but his troubles did not end.

Spike ran into problems with the film studios. Island Pictures had agreed to finance his next movie, *School Daze,* but they backed out when they thought that Spike was spending too much money. Columbia Pictures came to his rescue. The movie was filmed at Spike's college, Morehouse. But the college asked Spike to leave the campus after three weeks because it thought the film gave a bad impression of black people and black colleges.

To produce his movie *X*, Spike changed studios again. He had gone to Warner Brothers, but, when the film started going over budget, the studio refused to spend more money. Spike was determined to make the film, so he asked his friends for help. Many African-American celebrities such as Oprah Winfrey and Bill Cosby sent Spike enough money to finish *X*.

Spike has been called "one of the most original young filmmakers in the world."

Special Interests

- Spike is a fan of the New York Knickerbockers basketball team. He enjoys going to the games and meeting the players.
- Spike has not let fame and money affect him. He still lives in a small apartment in Brooklyn. He does not have a car or driver's license. He rides a bike and takes the subway.
- Besides making major motion pictures, Spike likes short film projects. He has made many music videos.

Sidney Poitier

Education: Western Senior High and Governor's High School.

Family: Married Juanita Hardy, 1950, divorced; married Joanna Shimkus, 1975. Has six children, Beverly, Pamela, Sherri, Gina, Anika, and Sydney.

Awards: Nominated for an Academy Award for *The Defiant Ones,* 1958; Silver Bear Award, Berlin Film Festival, 1958; Academy Award for *Lilies of the Field*, 1963; Lifetime Achievement Award, American Film Institute, 1992; Thurgood Marshall Lifetime Achievement Award, NAACP, 1993.

Personality Profile

Career: Actor and director.

Born: February 20, 1924, in Miami, Florida, to Reginald and Evelyn Poitier.

Growing Up

Sidney's parents were tomato farmers on Cat Island, a small island in the Bahamas. One day, when they had gone to Miami, Florida, to sell their crops, Sidney was born, two-and-a-half months early. The family returned to Cat Island where Sidney spent a happy childhood with his many brothers and sisters.

Sidney's parents exported their crops to the United States. In the 1930s, Sidney's father became ill, and Sidney had to leave school to help on the farm. To make matters worse, the American government had put a strict limit on the amount of tomatoes that could be brought into the country. With their main tomato market gone, Sidney and his family had to move to Nassau, the capital of the Bahama islands, to try and make a living.

In 1939, when Sidney was fifteen, he moved to Miami, Florida, to live with his brother, Cyril. Here Sidney experienced racism for the first time, and he felt lonely and confused. He got a job working as a messenger for a drug store but thought he could get a better job in New York City. He did not have the money to get to New York, so he sneaked on board freight trains and rode them all the way to Harlem. He arrived in New York with $1.50 in his pocket. Sidney found work as a dishwasher and slept on a roof.

During World War II, although he was only sixteen, Sidney lied about his age so he could join the U.S. Army. He served in a medical unit, and, when the war ended, he left the army and returned to New York.

"I saw my first movie at the age of ten-and-a-half and the first film I saw was a Western...[I wanted] to go to Hollywood where I thought those people were really working with cows."

S idney decided to become an actor. But when he first auditioned for a play at the American Negro Theater, the director kicked him off the stage, saying Sidney could not even read properly, let alone act.

Despite this setback, Sidney was determined to succeed, and, with the help of a friend, he improved his reading skills. Six months later, when he went back to the theater, the director agreed to train him in exchange for his doing backstage chores. Sidney's talent soon became apparent, and he starred in several plays including *Days of Our Youth* and *Strivers Road*.

Sidney on the set of the film version of **Raisin in the Sun.**

At age twenty-five, Sidney made his first film appearance when he starred in *From Whom Cometh My Help*, an army documentary. In 1950, Sidney appeared in his first major movie called *No Way Out*.

Film producers were impressed with Sidney and asked him to appear in many other movies. In one of his more popular films, *The Defiant Ones*, he played an escaped convict. Reviewers and audiences loved the movie, and Sidney was nominated for an Academy Award.

"As I saw it, in my career there was a real beginning for a breakthrough—not only for me, but for other blacks in film."

In 1963, Sidney played a handyman in the film *Lilies of the Field*. Critics raved about Sidney's performance, and when the Academy Awards were handed out, Sidney won an Oscar. He was the first African American to win an Academy Award.

Since then, Sidney has appeared in more than forty feature films. In 1972, he tried his hand at directing. His first movie was a western called *Buck and the Preacher*. Sidney has directed seven films since then. The most popular were *Stir Crazy* (1980) and *Hanky Panky* (1982).

Sidney won an Oscar in 1963 for his role in Lilies of the Field.

In addition to directing and acting in movies, Sidney has also performed on Broadway, the famous New York theater area. In 1959, he starred in *Raisin in the Sun*. He also directed the musical *Fast Forward* in 1985.

Accomplishments

1946 Appeared in the play *Days of Our Youth*.

1950 Feature film debut in *No Way Out*.

1958 Starred in *The Defiant Ones*.

1959 Starred in the play *Raisin in the Sun*.

1963 Starred in *Lilies of the Field*.

1972 Made directing debut with *Buck and the Preacher*.

1981 Wrote autobiography, *This Life*.

1995 Starred in the miniseries "Children of the Dust."

Overcoming Obstacles

omato farming was a risky business, and Sidney's parents had little money. Sidney wore clothes made of flour sacks and did not even know what ice cream or electricity were until he was ten. But throughout his childhood, his mother, Evelyn, told him to be thankful for what he had. She taught him to be truthful and polite – rules which Sidney still follows.

Sidney's first attempt at acting was a disaster. He had read an article in the newspaper that the American Negro Theater needed actors. Sidney thought this could be his big break and auditioned for a part. But the director kicked him off the stage because of his poor reading skills.

In 1993, Sidney and Harry Belafonte were presented with the Thurgood Marshall Award for their work in helping pave the way for better roles for minorities in the entertainment industry.

Sidney started practicing reading, and a friend helped him pronounce the difficult words. But reading well was not enough. Sidney still had a strong West Indian accent that most Americans could not understand. He went out and bought a radio. For six months, he listened to the radio and repeated everything he heard. From commercials to the newscasts, Sidney repeated the words, determined to change his accent. Gradually he began to speak with an American accent, and, when he returned again to audition for the theater, the director agreed to give Sidney acting lessons.

Up until this time, black actors were offered roles in movies only as servants or jazz musicians. But Sidney helped to change this with his moving performances. He was offered parts playing a doctor, a teacher, and a scientist. His powerful portrayal of these characters opened new doors for black actors in Hollywood. Still, some African Americans, fighting for better civil rights for black people, criticized Sidney for taking the same type of roles. They said he always played a successful black hero and did not show how many African Americans really lived.

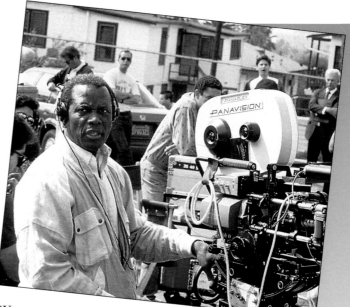

Besides acting, Sidney has also directed many projects.

Sidney partially retired in the early 1980s. He was still a popular actor, but he wanted to try new things, including writing. He published his autobiography, *This Life,* and produced another book called *The Films of Sidney Poitier*. When he tried to return to acting, his movies were not well received by the critics who felt that his skills were rusty. Sidney continued to make and direct movies despite the criticism. In 1995, at age seventy-one, he starred in a four-hour television miniseries called "Children of the Dust."

Special Interests

- Sidney knows a lot about the entertainment industry. In 1994, the Walt Disney Co. decided to make use of his knowledge when they elected him to their board of directors.
- Sidney likes to take acting jobs that have something good to say about life. He is not necessarily interested in how much money he can make.

Pearl Bailey

At first, Pearl wanted to be a schoolteacher, but her interest in show business was sparked when she was fifteen.

Music and singing were a large part of Pearl's childhood in Virginia in the 1920s. Her father was a minister with the House of Prayer, and, by the time she was three, Pearl was singing and dancing in her father's church. When her parents divorced, Pearl moved to Philadelphia, Pennsylvania, with her mother.

At first, Pearl wanted to be a schoolteacher, but her interest in show business was sparked when she was fifteen. She won an amateur contest at the Pearl Theater in Philadelphia. The prize was five dollars and a chance to perform for two weeks at the theater. Pearl was also promised thirty dollars a week, but she was never paid because the theater soon closed down.

Pearl left school to tour with vaudeville groups. She sang and danced in the coal-mining towns across Pennsylvania during the Depression. There was a lot of poverty and unemployment across the country. Pearl was paid only fifteen dollars a week, but she loved her work and decided to risk a career in show business. In 1941, Pearl had her big break. She was asked to perform at the famous Blue Angel night club in New York City.

During World War II, Pearl toured the military bases, entertaining the troops with her singing and dancing. She began working with big band groups and with famous jazz musicians. Her audiences loved her deep voice and warm personality, and they began calling her Pearlie Mae.

At age thirty-six, Pearl became a film star when she was cast in *Carmen Jones*. Again she was a hit and was offered many other roles. She appeared with well-known actors of that time including Harry Belafonte, Bob Hope, and Sammy Davis, Jr.

Pearl landed her biggest role when she was forty-nine. She was hired to perform in *Hello, Dolly!*, in a production featuring an African-American cast. Pearl became a star and was often asked to perform at the White House.

Pearl has performed on many television shows and has made several records with well-known bands. She was also the voice of the owl in the Disney movie *The Fox and the Hound*, the story of two friends who did not know they were supposed to be enemies.

Personality Profile

Career: Singer, actor, comedian, and author.

Born: March 29, 1918, in Newport News, Virginia, to Joseph and Ella Bailey.

Died: August 17, 1990, Philadelphia, Pennsylvania.

Education: B.A., Georgetown University, 1985.

Awards: Donaldson Award as the best newcomer on Broadway, 1946; Entertainer of the Year, *Cue* magazine, 1967; Special Tony Award, 1968; March of Dimes Award, 1968; Woman of the Year, USO, 1969; Heart of the Year, American Heart Association, 1972; Medal of Freedom, 1988.

During the last years of her life, Pearl turned her talents to writing. She wrote two books about her life: *The Raw Pearl* (1968) and *Talking to Myself* (1971). She also wrote *Pearl's Kitchen* in 1973. Her last book, *Between You and Me*, was published in 1990.

Late in her life, Pearl decided to finish her education because she had never completed high school. She enrolled at college, and, at sixty-seven, she graduated with a B.A. from Georgetown University in Washington.

In 1990, Pearl died of heart disease at age seventy-two. Two thousand people attended her funeral, and millions mourned the death of this wonderful person and entertainer.

Accomplishments

1933	Won an amateur competition at the Pearl Theater in Philadelphia; won a dance contest at the Jungle Inn in Washington, D.C.
1941	Performed for the armed forces.
1943	Began touring with well-known bands such as Count Basie and Noble Sissle.
1944	Solo performer at the Village Vanguard in Washington, D.C.
1946	Acted in the Broadway show *St. Louis Woman*.
1954	Starred in the musical *House of Flowers*.
1967	Starred in *Hello, Dolly!*
1968	Published her autobiograpy, *The Raw Pearl*.
1971	Published *Talking to Myself*.
1973	Published *Pearl's Kitchen*.
1975	Appointed special U.S. representative at the United Nations.
1990	Published *Between You and Me*.

Dick Gregory

He learned that by making jokes he could get people to laugh with him instead of at him.

Dick was raised in St. Louis, Missouri, by his single mother. The family lived in extreme poverty with no hot water and often no food or electricity. Dick helped support the family by shining shoes and doing odd jobs. Dick was often teased because he was poor and skinny. He learned that by making jokes he could get people to laugh with him instead of at him.

Because he knew that team members could get hot showers everyday, Dick wanted to try out for his high school track team. The coach did not think that Dick was good enough and refused even to let him try out. But Dick was determined to make the team, and he started running around the city to get in shape. A year later, the coach accepted him. Dick was soon setting track records, and, in his senior year, he became captain of the track and cross-country teams. He was also class president.

In 1951, Dick received a track scholarship to attend Southern Illinois University where he continued to set running records. In his spare time, he was a comedian at some of the university's variety nights. Dick loved the experience.

Personality Profile

Career: Comedian, nutritionist, and civil rights activist.

Born: October 12, 1932, in St. Louis, Missouri, to Presley and Lucille Gregory.

Education: Attended Southern Illinois University, 1951 to 1953, 1955 to 1956.

Awards: Winner of the Missouri Mile Championship, 1951 and 1952; Outstanding Athlete award, Southern Illinois University, 1953; Ebony-Topaz Heritage and Freedom award, 1978; honorary doctorate of humane letters, Southern Illinois University, 1989; awarded the key to the city of St. Louis; has received more than one hundred civil rights awards.

Two years later, when he was twenty-one, Dick was drafted into the army. Dick still enjoyed telling jokes, but one day he went too far when he poked fun at a colonel. The colonel was angry and told Dick that he would have to win that night's talent show or be jailed. Dick won the show and was transferred to the army's entertainment division.

After his discharge from the army, Dick went to Chicago to become a comedian. Work was scarce, and he had to work at odd jobs to make ends meet. When he was twenty-six, Dick opened his own night club called the Apex. The club closed in less than a year, but Dick was not ready to give up.

The next year, he rented the Roberts Show Club in Chicago and organized a party for the Pan American Games. Dick acted as master of ceremonies for the party, and the evening was a big success. The owner of the Roberts Club thought Dick was so talented that he made him his regular host. This gave Dick a chance to meet and learn from other famous comedians.

Dick got his big break at the Playboy Club when he was called to fill in for a sick comedian. At first, the owners of the club did not want Dick to go on because he was black. They felt that the white audience would not like him. Dick refused to leave and went on stage where he was met with insults. Instead of getting angry, Dick started to make jokes about the insults. The audience loved him, and soon Dick was a regular at the club. He was asked to appear in other clubs and on television. He was a hit!

Dick was also active in the civil rights movement, participating in marches and raising money for several civil rights organizations. In 1966, he was a candidate for mayor of Chicago, and, two years later, he ran for U.S. president as a candidate for the Freedom and Peace Party.

In the late 1960s, Dick ended his career as a comedian. He had become interested in nutrition and began talking at schools and universities about the importance of healthy eating. In 1984, he founded his own health company, Dick Gregory Health Enterprises, to provide information on proper diet and exercise. In his spare time, Dick runs in marathons.

Accomplishments

1954 Assigned to the U.S. Army's Special Services entertainment division.	**1961** Featured comedian at the Playboy Club, appeared on television and in other night clubs.
1958 Opened the Apex comedy night club in Chicago.	**1984** Founded Dick Gregory Health Enterprises in Chicago.
1959 Master of ceremonies at the Roberts Show Club in Chicago.	

Lena Horne

They had very little money, and Lena had to work to help the family.

Lena was raised in Brooklyn, New York. In 1920, when she was three, her father moved out of the house. Lena's mother left to pursue an acting career, and Lena was placed in the care of her grandparents. When she was seven, Lena moved back with her mother.

Because of her mother's career, Lena and her mother moved around a lot. They lived in Philadelphia, Miami, Macon, and Atlanta. When Lena's mother became sick and could not work, they returned to New York. They had very little money, and Lena had to work to help the family. She found a job as a dancer at the Cotton Club night club in Harlem. Even though she was paid only twenty-five dollars a week, she decided to spend part of her pay on music lessons.

In 1935, at age eighteen, Lena left the Cotton Club to join Noble Sissle's Society Orchestra in Philadelphia, Pennsylvania. Lena soon received other musical work and got her first big break in 1940 when Charlie Barnett, who led an all-white band, made her his lead singer. The next year, Lena was the featured singer at some of the most famous night clubs in New York City. She also dated boxing champion Joe Louis. Her fame was growing.

Lena moved to Hollywood, California, to sing at the Trocadero Club. When she was twenty-five, Lena became the second African-American woman to sign a contract with a Hollywood movie studio.

Lena continued to be a popular singer. She was one of the highest-paid African-American entertainers of the 1940s, receiving $1,000 a week from the movie studio and up to $10,000 a week from night clubs and theaters.

During the 1950s and 1960s, Lena's career soared. She appeared in movies, theater, television, and performed all over the world. She was also active in the civil rights movement. In 1965, Lena published her autobiography, *Lena*.

Personality Profile

Career: Entertainer, singer, and actor.

Born: June 17, 1917, in Brooklyn, New York, to Teddy and Edna Horne.

Education: Girls' High School, dropped out at age sixteen.

Awards: Page One Award, New York Newspaper Guild; Black Filmmakers Hall of Fame; Special Tony Award for distinguished achievement in theater, 1980; Grammy award, 1981; Kennedy Center Honor for Lifetime Contributions to the Arts, 1984; Raul Robeson Award, Actor's Equity, 1985; *Ebony's* Lifetime Achievement Award.

The early 1970s were very difficult for Lena. Her father, who had returned to help her during her success in Hollywood, died during the summer of 1970. A few months later, her son, Teddy, died of kidney disease. In April, 1971, Lena's husband, Lennie, died. Lena rarely appeared in public during the years after these tragedies. But in 1974, at age fifty-six, Lena was back performing on stage and in movies.

Lena had said she would do her last performances in 1980. But she decided to come out of retirement the next year to perform in the play *Lena Horne: The Lady and Her Music*. It was the longest-running one-woman show in New York. She was sixty-four years old.

Accomplishments

1933 Became a dancer at the Cotton Club in Harlem, New York.	**1942** Signed movie contract with Metro-Goldwyn-Mayer (MGM) in Hollywood.
1939 Starred in the song and dance show *Blackbirds of 1939* in New York City.	**1957** Performed in *Jamaica*, her first Broadway show.
1940 Became lead singer for Charlie Barnett's band.	**1965** Published her autobiography, *Lena*.
1941 Became featured singer at the Cafe Society Downtown in New York City.	**1981** Performed in the drama *Lena Horne: The Lady and Her Music*.

James Earl Jones

James was born on his grandparents' farm in Arkabutla, Mississippi, in 1930. Times were tough during the Great Depression of the 1930s, and James's parents were forced to leave the farm in search of work while he stayed with his grandparents. His father, Robert, was a boxer and actor, while his mother, Ruth, was a tailor. James knew his father only from telephone calls and saw his mother only when she returned for visits. James felt very lonely, but he kept himself busy hunting, fishing, and doing chores on the farm.

To escape the racism in the South, James's grandparents moved to Michigan. It was a difficult move for James. He felt he did not fit in with his new surroundings and began to stutter. One of his teachers suggested he memorize speeches and enter speaking contests. The idea worked. Not only did James overcome his stutter, but he also developed a powerful speaking voice.

James felt very lonely, but he kept himself busy hunting, fishing, and doing chores on the farm.

After high school, James received a full scholarship to attend the University of Michigan. He first studied medicine but later switched to theater. In 1953, he graduated with a degree in drama. James was drafted into the army for two years. After his term ended, James thought of following a full-time career in the army. His commanding officer suggested he try civilian life before making up his mind. So James went to New York City and took acting classes, knowing he could return to the army if he did not find success as an actor. He found small acting jobs and polished theater floors to earn extra money.

In 1957, James got his big break. He was given a part in the play *Wedding in Japan*. After that he was rarely out of work. He was willing to try any role no matter how small. He started his long career with the New York Shakespeare Festival in a non-speaking role as a spear carrier, and, four years later, he starred in the play *Othello*. That year he appeared in thirteen plays.

With his reputation as a stage actor growing, James got some small roles on television. He appeared on "The Defenders" and "East Side/West Side." His first movie role was the bombardier in *Dr. Strangelove*. He later became the first black man to receive a continuing role in a soap opera, playing the doctor in "As the World Turns."

Personality Profile

Career: Actor.

Born: January 17, 1931, in Arkabutla, Mississippi, to Robert Earl and Ruth Connelly Jones.

Education: B.A., University of Michigan, 1953; diploma from the American Theater Wing, New York City, 1957.

Awards: Numerous awards including: Obie Awards for Off-Broadway work, 1962, 1965; Tony Awards for best actor, 1969, 1987; Academy Award nomination, 1970; Emmy award, 1991.

James received national attention for his role in *The Great White Hope*, a play about the life of boxer Jack Johnson. James desperately wanted to play the lead. He trained at gymnasiums to build up his muscles and worked with boxing coaches. He got the part, and the play opened on Broadway in New York in 1968. James was nominated for a Tony Award for the role. *The Great White Hope* was later made into a movie starring James, and he was nominated for an Academy Award for his role in 1970.

Throughout the 1980s and 1990s, James performed in a variety of stage, television, and film productions. Some of his memorable movie roles include the voice of Darth Vader in all three *Star Wars* movies, a writer in *Field of Dreams*, and a CIA chief in *Patriot Games*.

Accomplishments

1957 Appeared in the stage production *Wedding in Japan*.

1962 Appeared on the television series "The Defenders."

1964 Starred in the stage production *Othello*; appeared in movie *Dr. Strangelove*.

1967 Starred in the play *The Emperor Jones*.

1968 Starred in the play *The Great White Hope*.

1970 Starred in the movie *The Great White Hope*.

1974 Starred in the play *Of Mice and Men*.

1977 Was the voice of Darth Vader in the movie *Star Wars*.

1979 Appeared in television miniseries "Roots: The Next Generation,", and the television series "Paris."

1990 Appeared in movie *Field of Dreams*.

1992 Appeared in movie *Patriot Games*.

1994 Was the voice of Mufasa in *The Lion King*.

1995 Appeared in movie *Jefferson in Paris*.

Diana Ross

By the time she was six years old, Diana knew she wanted to be a singer.

Diana learned to sing in the choir at the Olivet Baptist Church in Detroit, Michigan. She also sang at home with her parents. Her mother loved music, and Diana would often sit with her as she listened to famous musicians such as Billie Holiday. Whenever the family had visitors, Diana's parents would ask her to sing. By the time she was six years old, Diana knew she wanted to be a singer.

Diana performed in many elementary school programs and continued to sing in high school. She and several friends sang at weekend social events. Diana was asked by three girls in her neighborhood to join their singing group. They called themselves the Primettes and performed at local parties, dances, churches, and clubs.

The Primettes asked Berry Gordy, the president of Motown Records, to give them an audition, but he told them to finish high school first. The Primettes continued to sing, and soon they received a recording contract with Lu Pine records in Detroit.

After the girls finished high school, one of the singers left the group, and the remaining three signed a contract with Motown. First they sang back-up for other singers. In 1962, Berry renamed them the Supremes, and they began recording their own albums. At first the Supremes were not very successful, but when their music became more upbeat and Diana's voice was featured, they became a hit. Their song "Where Did Our Love Go?" reached the top of the record charts. It was the start of an incredible rise to stardom. The Supremes had twelve number-one songs, sold over fifty million records, and appeared on many television shows and in clubs around the world.

Diana wanted to be the star of the group. She studied drama and watched how other female artists performed. The extra work paid off, and, by the time Diana was twenty-three, the group was renamed Diana Ross and the Supremes. Soon Diana was appearing on television shows by herself. Her last appearance with the Supremes was on January 14, 1970.

Personality Profile

Career: Singer, actor, and business person.

Born: March 26, 1944, in Detroit, Michigan, to Fred and Ernestine Ross.

Education: Dwyer Junior High School; Cass Technical High School.

Awards: Female Entertainer of the Year, NAACP, 1970; Grammy award, 1970; Best TV Special of the Year, Image Awards, 1971; Entertainer of the Year Award, Cue Awards, 1972; Golden Apple Award, 1972; Gold Medal Award, *Photoplay*, 1972; Golden Globe Award, 1972; Academy Award nomination, 1973; inducted into the Rock and Roll Hall of Fame.

Between 1970 and 1984, Diana produced thirty-one record albums, often teaming up with other superstars such as Stevie Wonder and Michael Jackson. In 1972, Diana made her film debut as Billie Holiday in *Lady Sings the Blues*. Billie was the singer Diana and her mother loved to listen to when Diana was a child. She also appeared in *Mahogany* (1975) and *The Wiz* (1978).

In 1977, Diana established her own recording company, Diana Enterprises. Its success led to other business ventures such as RTC Management Company which manages other entertainers. She also formed Anaid Films which produces movies, and started JFF (Just For Fun) Enterprises to sell cosmetics and fashions. Diana formed several publishing companies. She also set up the Diana Ross Foundation to help charities. In 1989, Diana became a director of Motown Records. In this new role, she can help talented, young, African-American musicians get a chance.

Accomplishments

1962 Signed with Motown Records as a member of the Supremes.	**1970** Began a solo career.
1963 Released first album, *Meet the Supremes*.	**1972** Acting debut in *Lady Sings the Blues*.
	1977 Established Diana Enterprises.
1964 First number one single, "Where Did Our Love Go?"	**1981** Signed with RCA Records.
1967 Group was renamed Diana Ross and the Supremes.	**1989** Returned to Motown Records as a director.

Tina Turner

Although she was the youngest member of her church choir, she took the lead in all the upbeat songs.

Tina, who was born Anna Mae Bullock on November 26, 1939, spent her first two years on a farm in Nutbush, Tennessee. When she was only two, her parents left the farm to work in a factory in Knoxville. Anna Mae and her older sister, Alline, were separated, and each was sent to different grandparents. Anna Mae lived with her grandmother Mama Roxanna who was strict and unloving.

When Anna Mae was six, she and Alline returned to live with their parents, first in Flagg Grove and later Spring Hill. But Anna Mae's childhood was not happy. Her parents had many arguments, and she felt her sister, Alline, was her mother's favorite. But Anna Mae loved to sing. Although she was the youngest member of her church choir, she took the lead in all the upbeat songs.

When her parents divorced, Anna Mae lived with her father until he remarried and moved to Detroit. Then she went to live with her mother in St. Louis, Missouri. Life in the city was exciting for sixteen-year-old Anna Mae. She began wearing make-up and going to night clubs with Alline and her girl friends. At the Manhattan Club she met Ike Turner, the leader of the popular band The Kings of Rhythm. When he heard Anna Mae sing, he was so impressed that he asked her to join his act. She first performed under the name of Little Ann.

After graduating from high school, Anna Mae moved into Ike's house. In 1960, they had a son, Ronald Renelle, and later married. They recorded "A Fool in Love" in 1960. It was an instant hit and reached number two on the rhythm and blues chart. Ike decided to build his band around Anna Mae. He changed her name to Tina, and the band was renamed the Ike and Tina Turner Revue and became one of the hottests acts of its time.

During the sixties and seventies, the band toured the United States and Europe, singing a mix of blues, rock, and gospel music. In 1965, Tina recorded "River Deep, Mountain High." Although a failure in the United States, the song was extremely popular in Europe. The band, featuring Tina's singing, became the opening act for the Rolling Stones' 1966 European tour.

After a while, Ike and Tina's relationship began to fall apart. She was upset that he controlled all the band's business affairs. He was also an abusive husband, and just before a concert in 1976, he violently beat her. Tina divorced Ike, took a year off, and then struck out on a solo career.

The next few years were difficult. Tina performed in small night clubs, and an album she released in 1978 sold poorly. After the Rolling Stones asked her to join them on their 1981 U.S. tour, Tina again became a hit in America. In 1984, she was a special guest on Lionel Richie's U.S. tour. Later that year, Tina produced the album *Private Dancer* which was a great success and won Tina four Grammy awards. It sold more than eleven million copies around the world.

In 1985, Tina appeared in the movie *Mad Max: Beyond the Thunderdome* in which she sang the hit "We Don't Need Another Hero." The next year, Tina released the album *Break Every Rule*, her biggest-selling album to date. She continued traveling around the world, giving concerts on every continent. During her 1987-88 world tour, Tina's performance in Brazil drew a crowd of 182,000 fans — one of the largest concerts in music history. Now over fifty years old, Tina has stopped touring but still performs at concerts and appears on television and in movies.

Accomplishments

1960 Released debut song "A Fool in Love" with Ike Turner and formed the Ike and Tina Turner Revue.

1966 Recorded solo hit "River Deep, Mountain High."

1975 Appeared in the movie *Tommy*.

1978 Released solo debut album *Rough*.

1983-84 Embarked upon a European tour.

1984 Appeared as a special guest on Lionel Richie's American tour; released album *Private Dancer*.

1985 Appeared in the movie *Mad Max: Beyond the Thunderdome*; released hit single "What's Love Got to Do with It?"

1986 Released album *Break Every Rule*; published her autobiography, *I, Tina, My Life Story*.

Index

3 4 5 6 7 8 9 0 Printed in the United States 4 3 2 1